AF316727

This book is dedicated with
appreciation to my dear family; love to my mother Leah and my father Eliyahu;
my greatest wish for life's fulfillment to Yarin, Liran, Ido, Guy, Roni and
Assaf; my gratitude to all those who contributed to the realization of this
book, and special thanks to the illustrator,
Jorge Catacora.

ISBN: 978-0-9883020-9-9 (Paperback)
ISBN: 978-965-92961-1-8 (Hardcover)

Library of Congress Control Number: 2020923857

Illustrated by Jorge Catacora
www.jcatacora.com

Translated by Yael Valier
Bible verses sourced from: https://www.mechon-mamre.org

Easy to Print Publishing
www.karenashram.com

Dear parents and educators,

The Jewish people all over the Diaspora and in Israel may be divided into different streams of Judaism, which have developed different approaches to Jewish education, influencing the way we celebrate Jewish holidays on the national, religious, and societal level.

Nevertheless, the Jewish holidays feature a common thread of shared values, historical leaders, symbols, foods, blessings, and prayers that support their traditions and facilitate their transmission to the next generation.

The source for most of the holidays and festivals is the Torah itself. Some holidays were added by the sages, and several developed over time. Their dates are fixed by the Jewish calendar. In childhood, and well into our adult lives, the holidays help us feel connected and unified, conferring common societal values upon us.

This book takes the reader on an adventure through the Jewish people's most important holidays. By gaining familiarity with the holidays, children are exposed to Jewish values and witness the cycle of festivals, with its phenomenon of renewal that parallels that of nature. Tu Bishvat, for example, reflects a tree's cycle through the year and the planting of new saplings; Pesach is the time of the coming of spring and the blossoming of nature, and Shavuot welcomes the harvest time.

This book enables children's understanding of different customs that are rooted in historical sources, religion, and nature, and plants the seeds of identification and belonging, which goes hand in hand with the acquisition of values, such as unity, compassion, positive human relations, mutual help, and generosity.

Each of the book's holiday sections includes an informational question or a question that is food for thought. The answers to the informational questions do not appear in the book and they encourage the reader to seek further knowledge. The food-for-thought-questions create space for the readers' personal reflections on how they celebrate the holidays and how they find meaning in their practices.

The book also includes quotations from the Torah and from historical sources, and it is flavored with an Israeli spice.

Enjoy!

Yours with love,
Karen

SPINNY A DREIDEL'S ADVENTURES THROUGH THE JEWISH HOLIDAYS
Karen Ashram

It was the first night of Hanukkah. The sun had already set, the *hanukkiah* was sitting on the window sill, and the colorful candles shone brightly in the dark alleyway.

Mom, Grandma, Aunt Miriam, and all the other guests were sitting at the table, talking and eating the delicious fried holiday foods. Meanwhile, Ori was playing in his room with Spinny, the new dreidel he had received as a Hanukkah present.

Battery-powered Spinny was an energetic, mischievous, and joyful dreidel, who sang in Hebrew and accompanied himself with holiday music. Ori spun Spinny again and again, and Spinny happily sang and spun, until he got tired and wobbly. Eventually, he toppled over, but Ori helped him up and spun him one more time and then another. Spinny seemed very happy -- he danced and sang all the Hanukkah songs he knew without taking a break -- and Ori danced and sang right alongside him:

The Hanukkah candles had flickered out long ago. Grandma, Aunt Miriam, and the other guests had gone home, and the mouthwatering *latkes* (potato pancakes) and *sufganiyot* (jelly doughnuts) had all been eaten up.

"Ori, it's time to go to bed,"
called Mom.

Ori was quite tired, and a little dizzy too, but he couldn't resist playing with his wonderful new dreidel.

Spinny, however needed some rest! His head was spinning and his tunes had begun to sound scratchy.

Just then, when he was ready to nod off, Ori gave him a final spin. This time, it made him so dizzy that he had trouble coming to a stop.

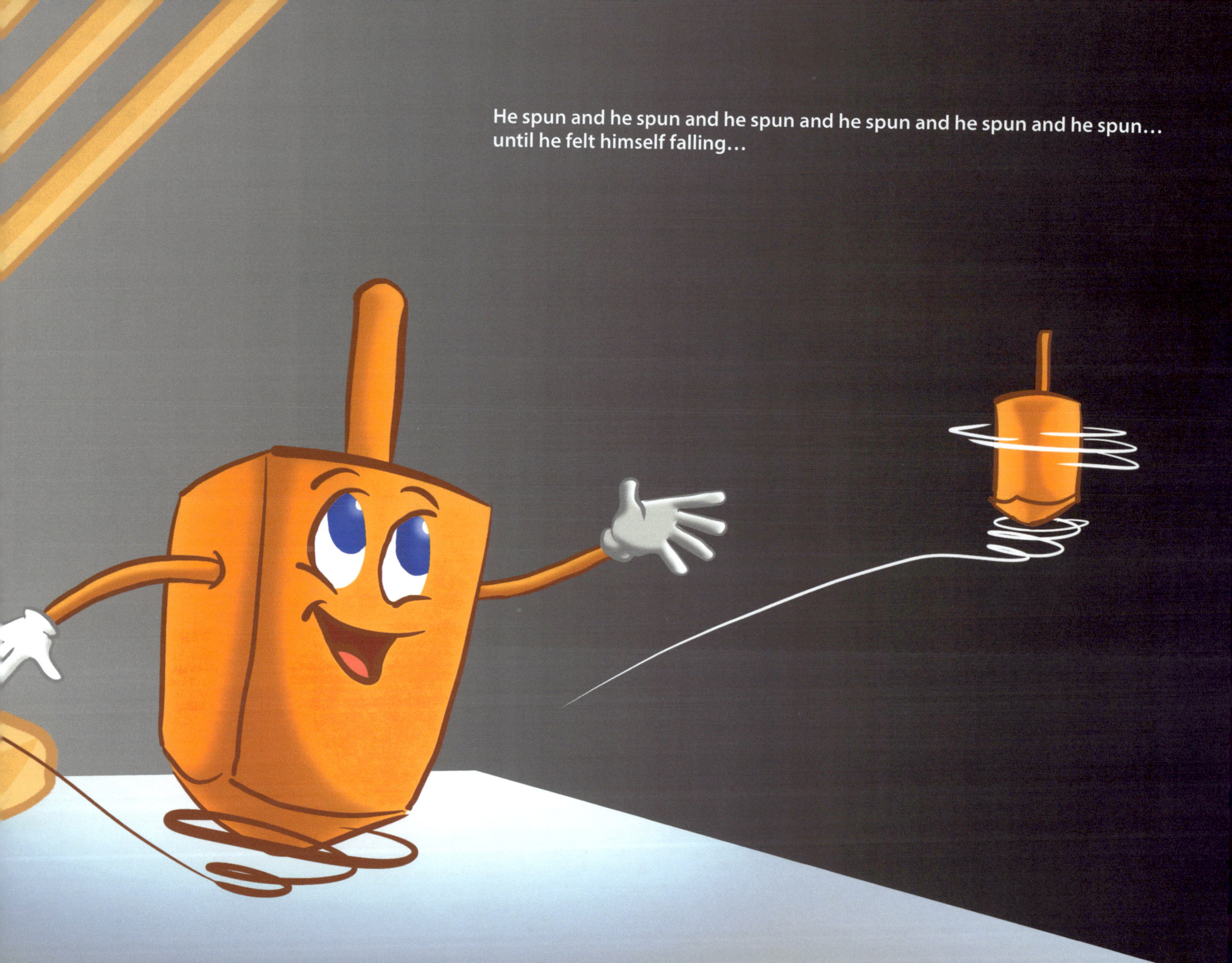He spun and he spun and he spun and he spun and he spun and he spun…
until he felt himself falling…

"Where am I? Hello? Can anybody hear me?"

"Ori? Ori?... Ori?"

No one answered. I was surrounded by silence. I lost my sense of direction.

Everywhere I looked was dark and unfamiliar.

Nervousness crept up on me and I began to worry—I have never liked being all alone.

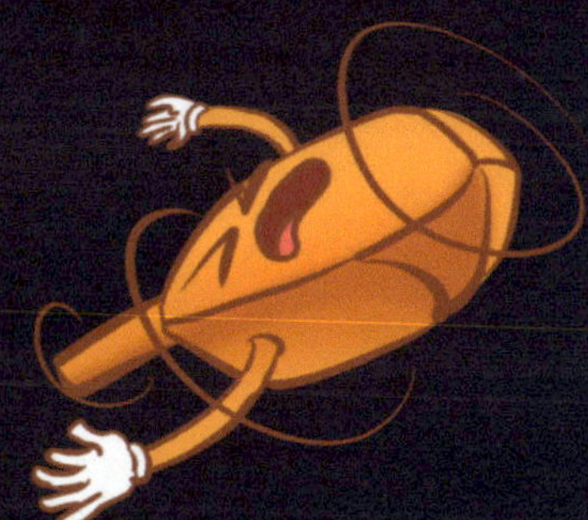

I missed Ori very much, but I realized that I didn't have time to sink into sadness or freeze with fear. I would have to draw out my happy feelings from deep inside and gather my strength in order to find my way back.

But back where? I remembered a bright place, the smell of sweet treats, and the sound of laughter and celebration.

And then a tune began to play and I listened, sure that it would show the way.

"Hello, dear dreidel, join us and come along to help us with our planting! Today we're honoring the New Year of the Trees, and wishing a happy holiday to all of nature.

"There is much work to do, but we are here with our friends and family to joyfully weed, rake, dig, and plant tiny saplings from which new trees will grow."

When you shall have come to the land and planted all manner of trees for food... (Leviticus 19:23)

Tu Bishvat, the fifteenth day of the month of Shevat, is a day of rejoicing here in the land of Israel. We make blessings over foods made of the seven special species of fruit and grain that grow in our blessed land, flowing with milk and honey.
We enjoy all sorts of dried fruits as well! With dates, raisins, olives, and figs, we have a real feast!"

I looked at the young trees, and turned to my new friends. "I had a great time helping with the planting, but now it's time for me to go on to the next holiday."

"Good luck, dear dreidel. You've helped us so, and it looks like you still have a long way to go!"

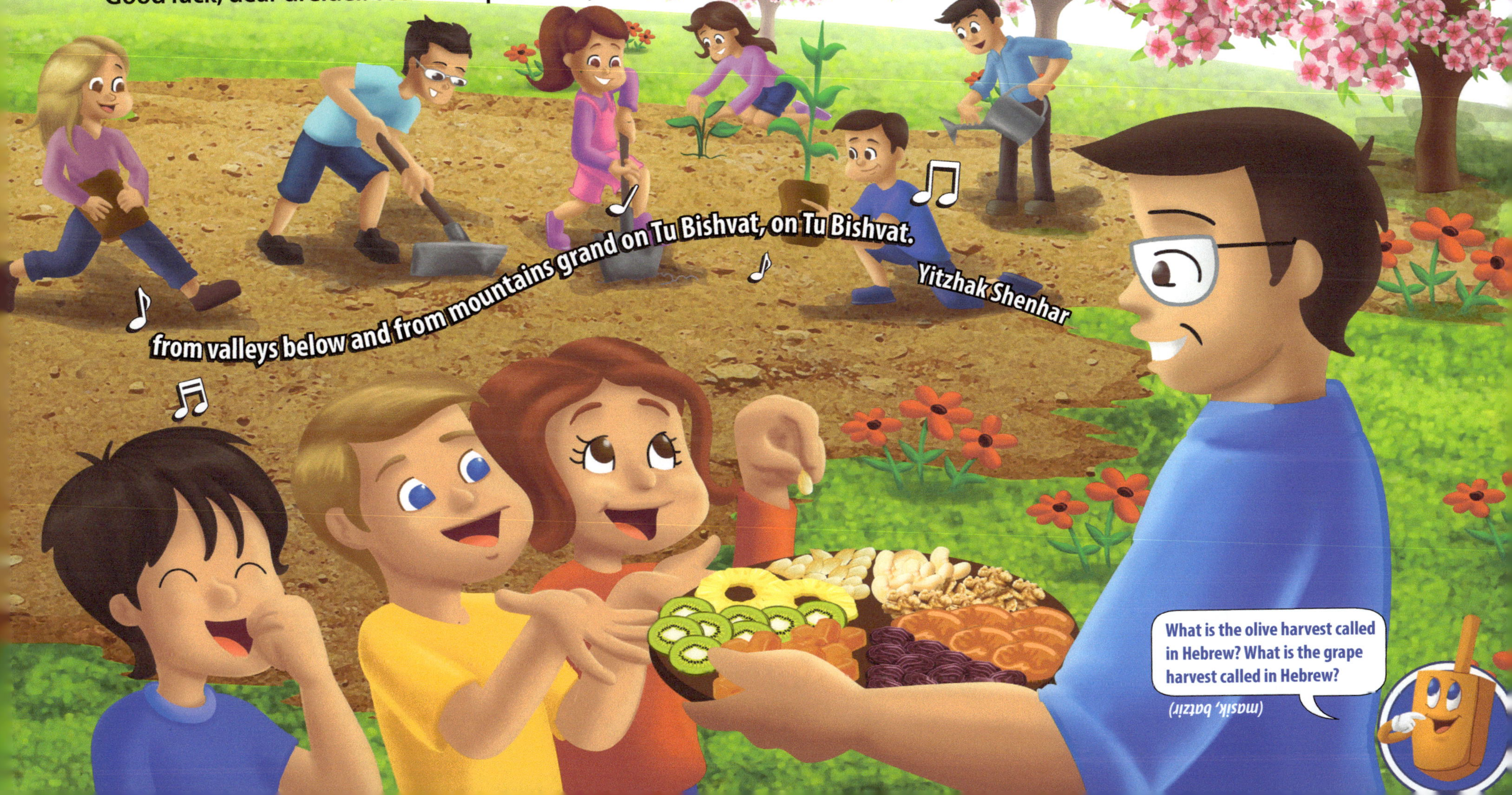

I went on my way, and I eventually heard happy sounds around me.

"Excuse me, everyone, but where are you going? What's happening here? I see a boy wearing a rooster's mask. Another boy has bear ears, and I see a girl with a glamorous cloak?!"

"Hello, dear dreidel! We are so happy! We've been getting happier and happier since the beginning of the month of Adar, and today is the happiest day of all! Come join our costume parade!

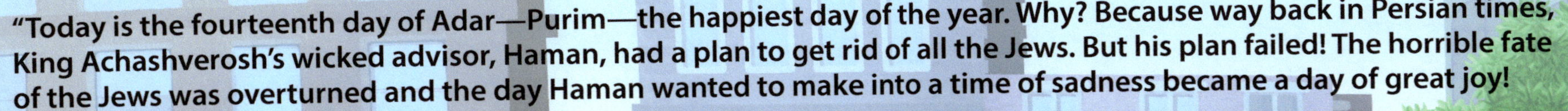

"Today is the fourteenth day of Adar—Purim—the happiest day of the year. Why? Because way back in Persian times, King Achashverosh's wicked advisor, Haman, had a plan to get rid of all the Jews. But his plan failed! The horrible fate of the Jews was overturned and the day Haman wanted to make into a time of sadness became a day of great joy!

The whole story is in the Book of Esther, which we read from a scroll, called a 'megillah.' Whenever the name 'Haman' is mentioned, we all make a lot of noise to drown out his name! We spin our noisemakers and stomp our feet to remember the wicked Haman and his final defeat.

We also prepare a feast, give charity to the needy, and make food packages for family and friends to express our affection and share the joy."

Again, I am amazed. "What a party! Thank you -- it's been fun. And now, I think it's time for me to move on."

Observe the month of Abib and keep the Pesach unto the L-RD thy G-d; for in the month of Abib the L-RD thy G-d brought thee forth out of Egypt by night. (Deuteronomy 16:1)

As I continued, I saw a group of people around a bonfire. I decided to speak up.

"Hello, hello everyone. I'm looking for my friend Ori. Do you happen to know where he lives?"

"Sorry, nice little dreidel, we don't know, and right now we are busy! We have a lot to do because Pesach, the spring festival and holiday of freedom, is coming soon. It's a joyous occasion!

We've cleaned our houses with great care and found all of the *hametz*, the leavening. Now all we have left to do is burn the last bits of bread, cake, and crackers left in our homes.

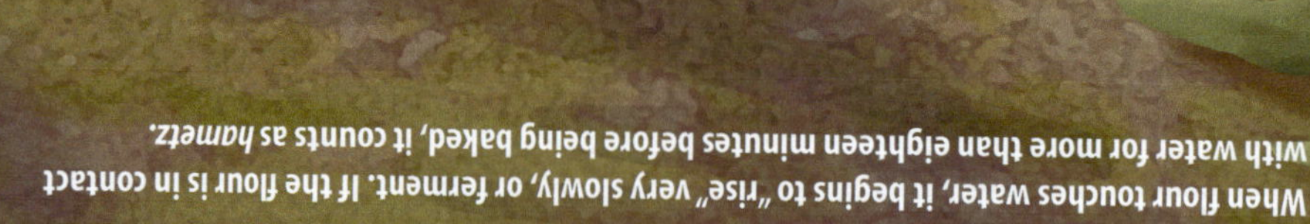

"Dreidel, you're invited for the special holiday Seder meal. Tonight, on the fourteenth of the month of Nissan, we will read the story of how the ancient Israelites left Egypt in our special holiday books, our *haggadas*. We'll learn about the ten plagues and stubborn king Pharaoh, who refused to let the Israelite slaves go!

"At the Pesach *Seder*, we'll make blessings over four glasses of wine or grape juice, we'll sing the *Ma Nishtana* song, and we'll eat the holiday foods—matzah, bitter herbs, sweet *haroset*, and *karpas*."

I set off on my way again. I see strange and spectacular lights in the distance – blue, red, yellow, green, orange, and even silver and gold. For a moment, they seem familiar and I am confused. Did I stumble on another happy holiday?

"You certainly did! It's the fifth day of the month of Iyar, the State of Israel's birthday—Independence Day! This is the day on which the independence of the new State of Israel was declared in 1948, and the Scroll of Independence was signed in a building called the Tel Aviv Museum, which today is called Independence Hall.

"From north to south, all of Israel makes merry and enjoys colorful fireworks.
Today, the State of Israel is _____ years old."

The Silver Platter by Natan Alterman
Translator: David P. Stern

...

Then a nation in tears and amazed at this matter
Will ask: who are you? And the two will then say
With soft voice: We--are the silver platter
On which the Jews' state was presented today

Then they fall back in darkness as the dazed nation looks
And the rest can be found in the history books.

"And you shall love the other as yourself—Rabbi Akiva says that this is a great Torah principle." (Jerusalem Talmud, the tractate of Vows, 9:4)

I moved on and came to another group of people around a bonfire. "Hello everyone. Are you burning the last of your *hametz*?"

"The last of our *hametz*? We finished that a long time ago -- Pesach has been over for almost four weeks! Today is the eighteenth day of the month of Iyar, which is also Lag Ba'omer—the 33rd day of the Counting of the Omer. It's a happy day, and we mark it around cheerful bonfires, with bows and arrows. It all reminds us that when the Land of Israel was under the rule of the Roman Empire, the Romans decreed that Jews could not learn Torah. But now we can!

"Rabbi Akiva and his students hid from the Romans and worked hard to keep spreading the light of Torah. When the Romans heard that Rabbi Akiva's student, Rabbi Shimon Bar Yochai, was teaching Torah despite their decree, they tried to hunt him down. To protect themselves and escape, Rabbi Shimon and his son Elazar hid in a cave in Peki'in, which is in the Galil, in the north of Israel, for thirteen years. They spent the entire time learning Torah, eating carobs from a carob tree that grew miraculously there, and drinking water from a spring whose source was right outside the cave's entrance. For all those years, Rabbi Shimon probed the deepest secrets of the Torah, and according to tradition, he delved into Jewish kabbalah, or mysticism, which later was written down in a famous book called the Zohar.

"Today is the anniversary of Rabbi Shimon Bar Yochai's death and crowds of people visit his grave on Mount Meron in the Upper Galil. They will gather together in music, song, and dance. Join us for the celebration, Dreidel! To be happy is a mitzvah."

"I'll stay for a while—what a merry celebration! I must go soon – to the next holiday of our nation."

Bar Yochai
By Rabbi Shimon Ibn Lavi
Translated by Avraham Sutton
Bar Yochai - fortunate are you, anointed with joyous oil [i.e. wisdom], over and above your companions.
Bar Yochai… You were anointed with the holy oil that flows down from the transcendent [source of mercy].
[Like the High Priest], you wore a holy crown that set you aside from other men, an aura of splendor bound eternally upon your head.
Bar Yochai…It was a comely dwelling that you found, on the day you ran away and escaped from the Romans.
[For thirteen years] you stood in the sand of the rocky cave - there you merited to your crown of splendor and radiance.

During the days of the counting of the *Omer*, we mourn for the 24,000 students of Rabbi Akiva who died in a plague. Some say that the tragedy may not have struck had the students respected each other more. During the *Omer*, it is customary to avoid haircuts and weddings. Some people even avoid listening to happy music. According to tradition, on the 33rd day of the *Omer*, the plague ended. As a result, the day ends the mourning period and is a happy occasion.

Suddenly, I see a mountain in my way. Silence. Masses of people stand at the foot of the mountain.

"Stay with us, Dreidel, and be careful not to climb the mountain. Today is the sixth day of the month of Sivan. It is the day when we received the Torah. We call the day 'Shavuot' which means 'weeks.' It commemorates the weeks of the Omer counting, beginning with the second day of Pesach and counting seven weeks until the 49th day. The 50th day is Shavuot.

Shavuot is one of the three holidays on which the People of Israel were commanded to walk in pilgrimage up to the Temple Mount in Jerusalem. On *Shavuot*, we were also commanded to bring the first of the year's produce to the Temple. What are the other two pilgrim festivals?

(Pesach and Sukkot)

"We'll gather together in the synagogue to hear the Ten Commandments read out loud from a Torah scroll. This is part of the holy Torah, with all its laws and rules that were given to the People of Israel at Mount Sinai.

"Many Jews stay awake all through the night of the holiday in order to learn Torah. It is our custom to read the biblical book of Ruth; to decorate our houses and synagogues with green plants; and to eat dairy products, cheesecake, blintzes, and sweets.

"Shavuot has other names, too: the Harvest Holiday and the Holiday of Produce. We fill our baskets with fruits and vegetables -- the produce of the land, we wear white clothing, and we decorate our heads with flower garlands."

The *Torah* was given to us on *Shavuot*. On that date, we decorate our houses and synagogues with branches and green plants in its honor because at the moment of the giving of the *Torah*, Mount Sinai was decorated with beautiful plants.

TISHREI

And in the seventh month, on the first day of the month, ye shall have a holy convocation: ye shall do no manner of servile work; it is a day of blowing the horn unto you. (Numbers, 29:1)

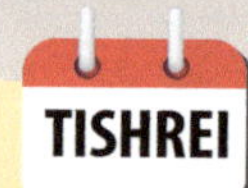

I hear trumpeting sounds…

“Hello, dear dreidel, have you come to observe Rosh Hashana with us?”

“Rosh Hashana?”

“Yes, on the first of the month of Tishrei, we’ll hear the blasts of the *shofar* that signal the beginning of a new year. That’s what Rosh Hashana means—'Head of the Year', or ‘New Year.’ This is the first day of the Ten Days of Repentance, during which the gates of remorse and forgiveness are open. This is a time of spiritual awakening and renewal, which ends at the locking of the gates of heaven at the end of the holiday of Yom Kippur. We even symbolically empty our pockets of our less-good deeds and thoughts into running water during a ceremony called, *Tashlich*.

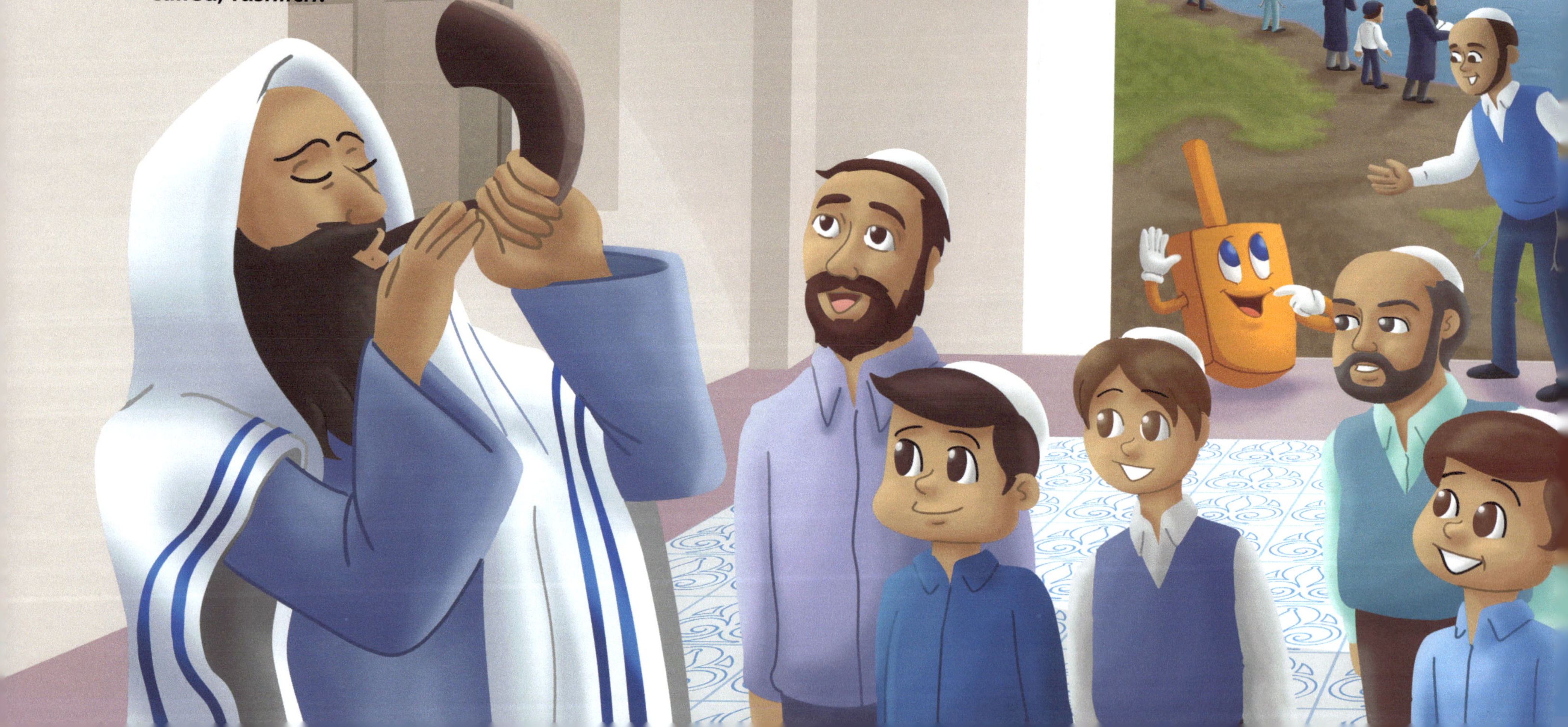

"Join us for the holiday meal! We'll express the hope that this year we will be the head (the leaders) and not the tail (the followers). We'll also dip apple pieces into honey. May this new year be sweet, happy, and full of exciting beginnings."

"Hmm, it's a special atmosphere and I'd love to help everyone get ready for the New Year, but it's time for me to continue on my way to the next holiday."

"And now we've arrived at the tenth day of Tishrei. It's Yom Kippur, a day to think about who we are and what we have done. It is a day of regret, making amends (that's apologizing, of course), and prayer from the depths of our hearts that we will be forgiven, hoping the future will bring each and every one of us a good and long life.

"Adults and children over the age of bar or bat mitzvah begin fasting in the evening, when the sun sets. This is the time during which the gates of heaven are open to prayers, pleas, requests, and responses. The next day, at the sound of the *shofar* blast after the final prayer, the gates close again and Yom Kippur ends."

"I've experienced prayer and repentance and felt things I've never felt before.
With faith in my heart, and curiosity, it's time for one holiday more."

Ye shall dwell in booths seven days; all that are home-born in Israel shall dwell in booths. (Leviticus 23:42)

I see many funny little huts topped by branches. Maybe I should take a peek to see how they look inside?

"Hello, dear guest, please join us in our sukkah. Hosting is a mitzvah. In fact, over the seven days of the holiday, we invite the following seven extra-special guests: the forefathers Abraham, Isaac, and Jacob, and the leaders Moses, Aharon, Joseph, and King David.

"Sukkot begins on the fifteenth of Tishrei, five days after Yom Kippur.

"These sukkah huts symbolize the way of life when the People of Israel wandered in the desert for forty years.
They also symbolize the clouds of glory that surrounded the people as they left Egypt, protecting them from the heat of day, the cold of night, and other hardships.

"The holiday of Sukkot is also called the harvest festival because this time of year is the season of the grain harvest. During the holiday, we are commanded to bind a palm branch, willow branches, and myrtle branches to each other, and we hold them together with an *etrog*, or citron—a special citrus fruit that looks like a lumpy lemon. When we have all four species in hand, we wave them and make a special blessing.

"Dreidel, would you like to help judge our competition for the most beautiful sukkah?"

"There are so many beautifully decorated sukkahs, how could you possibly choose? But now, I must move -- there's no time to lose!"

Our sages said the following:
The four species have different characteristics which represent the different kinds of people in our nation. We bind them together to show how important it is for us to be united despite our differences.

"Welcome dreidel is it your first time here? Join us for the reading!" Every Shabbat, we gather in the synagogue and read a section from one of the five books of the Torah. On the holiday of Simchat Torah, we read the last section, "This Is the Blessing," and complete our reading of all five books. Then we start again from the beginning, with the first section of the book of Genesis. We rejoice together, as we proudly parade with our Torah and begin the cycle of reading.

"On this day, the 22nd of Tishrei, we take out the Torah scrolls from the ark, their special cupboard, and we hold them as we dance around the reading platform, the bimah, at least seven times. Outside of Israel, the holiday is observed one day later. The first day is called 'Shmini Atzeret,' the 'Eighth Day of Assembly,' and the second day is called 'Simchat Torah,' the 'Joy of the Torah.' Together, we sing, dance, and praise: 'Be happy and joyful on Simchat Torah and give honor to the Torah!'"
The person who is honored with the first reading in the book of Bereishit is called the _______
(Chatan Bereishit)

Off I go again, looking for the way home. I stop and ask for
directions, rest for a moment, and sit on the side of the path.
I am tired, sad, and lonely.

Darkness has fallen and suddenly…wait,

I know those lights! I hear the sound of people laughing and there is a sweet smell in the air. Now I know! This is *my* holiday! The lights that I see shining are from the *hanukkiah*, the sweet smell is that of jelly doughnuts, and the laughter comes from children who are playing and spinning colorful dreidels.

"Ori? Ori? Are you there?"

"Is that you, Spinny? Yes, yes, I'm here!"

What a special Hanukkah miracle—I've found my way home! It is the 25th day of the month of Kislev, the Festival of Lights. On this day, two miracles happened: The Jewish Chashmona'im soldiers, who were very few, beat the mighty battalions of the Greek army, and one small pitcher of pure oil was found in the defiled Temple – at least it would light the menorah (the Temple's seven-branched candelabrum) for one day…
Yet astonishingly, the oil from that pitcher burned
in the menorah for eight days.

For that reason, we light Hanukkah candles for eight days, give each other gifts, play with colorful dreidels, and eat delicious fried foods. Our favorites are sufganiyot and latkes!

I am surrounded by light. I've banished the darkness and found my way home!

Ori and I are together again. We play and dance and sing Hanukkah songs. "I have a little dreidel, I made it out of clay, and when it's dry and ready, oh dreidel I will play…"

Hanukkah means "dedication" and the holiday was named for the re-dedication of the Temple when the Jewish Chashmonaim soldiers rebelled and defeated the Syrian Greek army. At that time, the Temple and the altar were re-dedicated for holy service.

What a fascinating trip through the Jewish holidays.
I've learned about so many traditions.

Every holiday and festival is special and unique, with
its own foods and symbols and its own mystique.

There are so many holidays when we gather in celebration. We share values and traditions from generation to generation.

Thank you for agreeing to come along. Let's meet again soon with revelry and song!

9 789659 296118